I Love My Sister

I Love My Sister

And a Christian Walk—
One Stiletto Step at a Time

Shemekia S. Samuels

WestBow Press books may be ordered through booksellers or by contacting:
WestBow Press
A Division of Thomas Nelson
1663 Liberty Drive
Bloomington, IN 47403
www.westbowpress.com
1-(866) 928-1240

ISBN: 978-1-4497-9916-8 (sc)
ISBN: 978-1-4497-9917-5 (hc)
ISBN: 978-1-4497-9915-1 (e)

Library of Congress Control Number: 2013911270

Printed in the United States of America.
WestBow Press rev. date: 07/09/13

Introduction

I cannot begin to tell you how amazing your life is meant to be. We all have been or are going through crevices in life where we know something is missing. However, we are either too afraid to release them, or when we do, we are so used to those ins and outs that we fall back into those same crevices.

What's your crevice? Are you pleased with it, or are you trapped by its taunting darkness? No matter what your answer is, you weren't made to exist in crevices let alone darkness. You are promised a life of light, sanity, and goodness, a life of power, love, and a sound mind. Day after day, year after year, your heart and mind ache for something great. Guess what? There's no more guessing necessary; the time is now. This book will give you the insights you need to live your life the way you were meant to.

I am no saint, I must admit, but what is a saint? A saint is just a sinner who fell down and got up. I can assure you that from my birth up until a few years ago, I lived a life of uncertainty, hurt, unfaithfulness, and darkness. Then came a time when I wanted a purpose, because how could I live day after day with just sore emptiness? I started a female care group called I Love My Sister, which aids in empowering, encouraging, and freeing women to share and understand others so they can understand themselves.

Men often jeer at us females, saying, "If a woman can't get along with or understand other women, hence herself, how can she understand us?" Think about it. When a man enters a roomful of men, it's amazing how quickly they find something—sports, cars, some new invention—to talk about. However, when a female walks into a room and sees other females, I guarantee you emotions will start to boil, including hate and jealousy. Egos start to flare, and there is tension that a knife could cut.

We women need to look into ourselves and realize we are meant to lift each other up; doing simply that will make us confident. We will be better people, better wives, better mothers, better workers—better in all the roles we manage. In I Love My Sister, we never forget to pray; we've found that prayer changes t h ings. We don't hold back because we've realized every area of our lives needs assurance, deliverance, and certainty.

Here is my empowerment to you, and I pray you will be blessed, uplifted, and released from your place of uncertainty, neglect, hurt, or whatever you may be struggling with. I pray you may be enlightened.

What Is Your Will, God?

Dear Lord, one evening, some classmates asked me what field I was going to do my master's degree in. I mentioned several areas as possibilities, but I honestly didn't know. I won't move until I know your will, Lord. Let me know your will for my life on this earth, because so many people have died never having tuned in to your will. So many have leaned just on themselves and have never found contentment. Our lives begin when we discover your will for us, Lord. When the first thing we reckon with is your plan for us, our lives will unfold.

Remember, no matter how impossible or unrealistic God's plan for you seems, it is designed for you, and it can happen. "When you approach a door that is very large, do not fear, because I will open it. When God opens the door, no man can shut it" (Revelation 3:7–8). We simply have to know that you are God. "Be still, and know that I am God; I will be exalted among the nations, I will be exalted in the earth" (Psalm 46:10).

Prayers and Fasting

I have prayed and fasted for my husband because I want him to have the faith that I have. He and I are one, and the whole unit has to be certain. There is no beauty in a rose if one petal is fresh but another is withered. We women are more mindful at times of grace and reverence, while some of our husbands are obviously far from God. My husband's plight is that he's not ready to be a Christian. He doesn't go to church on his own. If I'm at work, he will not take our son to Sunday school. Football season is an excuse not to go to church at all.

Open the door of salvation, Lord, and save them, because it's not easy when we are Christians and our spouses are far from God. Bless them in their jobs, O God, because getting jobs is not easy. I pray for supernatural breakthroughs in their jobs and your grace, unmerited favor, and peace to be on them. Save all men who believe it's "mushy" to become Christian. Bless them with your salvation first, and their hearts' desires will follow, because according to your Word, "Seek first the kingdom of God and his righteousness, and all things will be added to you" (Matthew 6:33)

I praise your name, God. You deserve everything. I can't thank you enough. Forgive me, because I feel I'm not worshipping you enough. You have done so much for me.

What can I do for you? I feel strong, but bits of me have doubt about what to do or what will happen in my life. I vow that if all things seem possible to man and we can thrive because of this so-called strength of ours, what about your mighty power and limitless strength? We sometimes feel bad and bold, like the Incredible Hulk, but after each high comes a low.

We need constant victory, Lord, and I'm praying for it. We cannot afford to rely on our strength as if we were battling flesh.

> "For our struggle is not against flesh and blood, but against the rulers, against the authorities, against the powers of this dark world and against the spiritual forces of evil in the heavenly realms" (Ephesians 6:12).

When we fight, the influence is deeper than we think. So heavenly Father, influence us, because you know us, you love us, and you give us never-ending strength. "I can do all things through Christ who strengthens me" (Philippians 4:13). Please don't take your Holy Spirit power away from us. All we need is your instinct of right and wrong. Lord, let us be sensitive to you, *please*. I seek your face right now.

Your Miracles

Bless us supernaturally. Give us breakthroughs. Heal us, Lord, heal us. I'm thinking of a coworker's aunt who died last year of uterine cancer, and now her mother has been diagnosed with the same thing. Heal her mother, Lord. I pray against that cancer in your name, Jesus. Work a miracle and save her because you are the Savior. Don't let my coworker grieve during this time that should be the happiest of all because she's getting married. Humble her and the rest of her family with your touch and deliverance. Be with them right now, Lord, and heal because you are a healer; let her be cancer free. I pray against the spirit of superstition and doubt, and I bless your name.

I occasionally work with children in the New York school system who have been diagnosed with behavioral problems and are taking medication. The diabetic children, Lord, can't have normal school days because they have to report to the medical room throughout the day. Lord, sickness is not from you. Diagnose them with health and strength, Lord, I pray in Jesus' name. I love and thank you in advance. I bless your name. *I love you.*

I pray for our son, that he will hear, grasp, understand, and be obedient. Cover him with your blood, and keep him.

His teacher once complained he was being disobedient, not following directions, and disturbing others. I always see improvement when I ask for your help, Lord, and I pray over him. I thank you for being with him and for the progress he's made.

Help us to continually pray for our children—in the morning, throughout the day, and at night—and help us rehearse psalms and the Lord's Prayer with them, Lord. We have to bring them up in righteousness, Lord, so they learn to call on your name, which is above all others, and it brings deliverance. El Shaddai! Adonai! This is the Hebrew for "God Almighty."

Lord, the Devil has a plan to make this generation of children obsolete, to silence your work and power, but we plead for your blood, Lord, to cover all the children in the world. We know and trust your unfailing love, truth, discipline, and protection over them.

Seeking God's Face in Everything, All Day

It is funny how things pan out day by day. I will never forget how one morning, I planned to leave at 7:00 a.m. to drop my son off at school because I had to reach the school where I worked by 8:00. I woke up and started cleaning. Women, don't we all often wake up with bursts of energy and start cleaning our houses before we head out? My husband thought I had an attitude, and I had to check myself before I got all defensive about his own attitude.

I think that the first thing we should do when we wake up is seek God's face. We should drop all sense of self to make room for God in our day, just like babies wake and immediately look for their nurturers. God's grace and mercy will set the tone for our days if the first thing we do is thank him and ask him to be present throughout the day with us. We let God know he is first, or so we think—we are really just reminding ourselves that he is first, and we allow his grace to carry us through the day. In most instances, that acknowledgment of him right when we wake will cancel all that the enemy has waiting for us through the day. We will have reminded ourselves God is first, and by so doing, the enemy learns that we know God is first and that the enemy is not welcome anytime; he will not have room to creep in.

But to continue about my plight that day, I took it on as my own, with no regard for the Most High. I went to two different schools before I found the one I was supposed to report to. I was supposed to go to 244 Tenth Street, but I ended up going to 244 Eleventh Street. I even thought to park a couple of blocks away and to take a bus to avoid traffic. I thank the female security guard who gave me directions; bless her family right now, Lord, in Jesus' name.

I thought to check another school to see if it was my assigned school, but thank you, Lord, for letting me press on, that is, press on the gas. I parked in the wrong parking lot and wasted money, a bad start to my day. So I know, dear God, that these little things matter. We take it for granted not to even call on you for things as simple as headaches; what can *Advil*, *Tyleno*l, or *Excedrin* do for us that you can't if we just acknowledge and believe in you?

I bless our Lord when I wake up in the morning, throughout the day, and at night. If we don't find the time to bless God, the enemy can put us in a state of loss—he blocks our minds with temptations, gives us false hope, and tries to ruin our days God has made. At the ends of our days, we feel lost, unproductive, and depressed, the "blessings" of the enemy.

Help us to not be naïve, God, but to trust and obey and be at one with you. I thank you, God, a father who will never abandon his children. You are here with us, and just as we thank our earthly fathers, we thank you, bless you, and seek your guidance from sunup to sundown.

Lord, I know you forgive those who ask forgiveness; you don't hold things against them. "Because of the Lord's great love we are not consumed, for his compassions never fail. They are new every morning; great is your faithfulness" (Lamentations 3:22–23).

My "Daniel Fast"

I did a twenty-one-day "Daniel Fast." On the last day of my fast, I felt that I was going to "miss" God. Like wow! *It's so over*, I thought, but I realized later that the fast had reconnected me to God.

I love you, God, and I thank you so much for this experience. Thanks to my coworker who recommended this fast. Thanks to Pastor Jentezen Franklin's book, which guided me through this worthwhile experience. I felt sad, I felt happy, but most important, I am still holding on to my faith and your promise, God. I am praying that you break generational curses, because not one man in my family is saved, and not one of my six young male cousins has a job. They all have a mentality that tells them they are owed something, and they are not persistent.

You know, Lord, before I had my son, I merely prayed for the men in my family, but after I had my son, another male in the family, I started praying against generational curses. I thank you for my son and the opportunity to pray for my family. Thank you, God. All glory to you. Thank you for the Holy Spirit. I love you, Lord.

Listening to God's Voice for Direction

During the summer, I went to the Willow Creek Global Leadership Summit and was truly inspired by every aspect of it. It is so amazing when as Christians we expand ourselves out of Sunday service and learn new things. I thank my church, Bronx Bethany Church of The Nazarene, for encouraging us to participate in this event. Thanks to Willow Creek for the event itself.

Lord, while I was at that summit, I thought to myself about what your will is for me. I know it has to do with kids, because I love children.

One lunch break, I decided to make a little fast to hear God's voice. Trust me, readers, when you make special time to hear his voice, it will be crystal clear. I sat in my car, missing the jerk chicken and beef patties, but I got a grip on myself. I started to pray, to ask God his will for me, and as plain as day, I got a vision to minister to young women like myself, to tell them the truth—where I've been, where I'm at—and simply about God. I felt happy to have gotten this vision, but I started wondering how this ministry would happen. I told a pastor about my vision, and he encouraged me; he said I could partner with his wife, who shared the same interest.

As time went on, I hesitated, I got excited, and I ignored this vision at different times. I wondered where to have it, whom to tell, and how it would work out. In this process, I realized that I always hosted fabulous get-togethers at my house for pleasure and that I should just be brave and host it myself. I wasn't in the habit of inviting just anyone to my house, however, and I wondered what my husband would say; I was afraid he would think I was crazy for inviting all kinds of people over, and I was afraid no one would come.

Well, I went ahead with my plan despite my fears; I fasted before the first meeting of I Love My Sister; I prayed that one hundred girls would attend; I prayed for direction and that it would go well. Five beautiful young women attended, and to my surprise, they eagerly wanted to know when the next meeting was going to be held.

Thank you, Jesus; it was a very honest and refreshing meeting. I thought if only we could get a TV network to broadcast our meetings. I mean, networks broadcast reality shows all the time with all sorts of behavior, so what about I Love My Sister, which could reach thousands of women who need to share their experiences and know that God is with them? When the time is right, if it's God's will, it will happen.

I thank you, Lord, for being my life, my air, my peace, my everything. I want you to bless the coworker of mine who encourages me to continue with writing, which is indeed a refreshing way to share and talk with you.

God in the Workplace

I work with a good group of nurses. Anyone who works in a group can sense when something is about to go down in that group. Two staff members had a heated incident with heated words and heated behavior. I wasn't there, so I can't vouch for what actually went on, but I felt bad about being a part of a unit in which something was always about to go down even though I am honored to work with premature babies. Apparently, my preceptor was a part of that confrontation, but I also liked the other woman involved, so the situation called for "hashtag awkwardness."

One of the women asked me if I believed she was pushy in any way when she was in charge, and I said no. If she had asked me if she had an issue about controlling her anger, from past events I've witnessed, I would have said yes. I like her, I think she is a nice person, but I feel she has an anger pot inside that boils over at times, and she probably has trust issues as well.

I pray, Lord, that you resolve these things for her and let your peace, confidence, and greatness flow on her. Our unit brings up arguments that took place five, even ten years ago, Lord. Help us to solve issues as we go so we can avoid reliving past turmoil. I pray this for all other work places and all areas of our lives because the Devil is such a liar.

He is the ruler of turmoil, war, secrets, devouring, divorce, and separation. Heavenly Father, give us the will to express ourselves in decent ways, to let go of the past, to let others receive us well, and to let us forgive them so you will forgive us.

I work with many different personalities; some are scared, others go by the book, some are timid, or bold, or rude, or genuine. I enjoy and appreciate our mixed pot, but one of my coworkers is a time bomb who can go off about anything at any minute. One day, I needed to take my patient's blood pressure, but my monitor wasn't working, so I had to borrow the one she had been using on her patient, who was in the next bed. When she came into the room, I felt so nervous, because my infant's blood pressure reading remained on her patient's machine; I hadn't "erased" the evidence. *Tick, tick, tick ...* I was waiting for the explosion.

"Who troubled my blood pressure monitor?" she asked in a way that made me feel an argument was on its way. Her tone escalated. I could have argued with her, asked her why she was so angry at times, or ignored her question, but I didn't. I confessed it was me. "A soft answer turneth away wrath, and grievous words stir up anger" (Proverbs 15:1).

Help us not to be hotheads, Lord, but to gather our thoughts and think before we speak or act.

Sharing the Lord with Others

Lord, I wanted to invite some coworkers to church. It was a bold step for me, because I felt afraid and ashamed to even talk about you, God. I felt that if I just kept you to myself and we engaged in rapport as needed, we'd be good, but if that's what the enemy wants, you clearly don't stand for that.

You want us to share the peace and joy you've brought us, to speak of what you've done for us so others know there is a way out of uncertainty, insecurity, hate, and oppression. I can cry, shout, rejoice, testify, and be so happy you brought me out of those.

Thank you for pastors such as Pastor Ronald Benjamin, Pastor Samuel Vassel, Pastor Carlene Reynolds, Pastor Richard Griffiths, Pastor Steven Furtick, Pastor Jentezen Franklin, Pastor John Hagee, Pastor Creflo Dollar, Pastor Joseph Prince, Pastor Joel Osteen, the pastors and speakers at Willow Creek Global Leadership Summit, and others. I have been blessed by their teaching. Their sermons gave me a view of how I can be free. If these people had not spoken, woe would be unto my soul, but because they spoke about you, I listened and got to know you better.

Help us Christians to not be afraid but be obedient and share you. Just as I got a piece of you through those preachers' testimonies, I pray in Jesus' name you will deliver my coworkers and readers from everything they are going through.

The one thing that separates us from God is sin, but Jesus died so all sins would be forgiven. If you want to be close to God and gain eternal life, believe that Jesus died for your sins and ask Jesus to come into your life as your Lord and Savior. It's is as simple as that—you will be saved, no shenanigans. God loves you, and it is not his will for you to die but to live eternally with him. You can go to heaven, or you can merit eternal death.

Thank you, Jesus, for the time we can use to repent, ask for forgiveness for our sins, read the Bible, pray, and draw continually closer to you.

We have to pray every moment and chance we get, even though our carnal natures encourage us to kill time and avoid reverence. We can be reverent anywhere—washing our hair, jogging, cooking, working, you name it. We can pray and seek God's face even on lunch breaks. We are all at different places in our walks with God, but God always knows and understands where we are, and he graces us through our walks.

I used to think that God was there only when we prayed, but I now realize God is with us always. I planned to dedicate a week's fast to him to seek his direction, be close to him, and hear his voice. In the past, I would dedicate a few days of a week's fast to my husband, some days to my son, and some days to my extended family, but this whole fast was dedicated to God. I was ignorant in spirit, thinking, *Okay, here's a fast. I'm just laying down different concerns in my life to him, and he has to answer, and then there will be a "slot" for him.*

I look back at that time in my life and realize I've truly learned from it, and I praise God for that. Because God is good, we have to involve him in all matters in our lives; we can't set up a wall in front of him and pull it down to let him in when we want to; he has no boundaries. We will not realize this, however, until we pray and revere him; he will then see that we want to be better and closer to him, and we will be pleasantly surprised how much in tune with him we become in the inner dance, joy, peace, and love God blesses us with.

The Trinity

You notice I have written about God, Christ, and the Holy Spirit? It's almost as if we're worshipping three people, right? Well, in a sense we are, but this three is actually one. God the Father created heaven and earth, everything in existence. Jesus Christ is God's Son, whom God created so we could relate to him as a human. You and I know that if God had come down to talk to us, we would have been too smitten by his superiority; whatever he would have told us would have gone in one ear and out the other. Being the supreme and wise God he is, he sent his flesh and blood, Jesus, to teach us his way.

God wanted someone to save the world by dying for our sins; if we believe this, we will not perish but will have everlasting life through Jesus Christ. Our poor, little minds can't begin to understand how much God loves us. There is no greater love, do you hear me? Okay, good.

Then there is Holy Spirit. You may ask why we need the Holy Spirit, but I ask why do we need tarot cards, psychics, or witchcraft? We all search for the truth, for guidance, but God has provided us with the Holy Spirit for this reason. The Bible offers us great insight and rewarding explanations about the nature of the Trinity, so I encourage you to read it.

Imprisoned by Our Minds

Where are you mentally today? What particular reasoning, realizing, or doing space are you in right now? I have thought I could do anything I wanted. If I decided to start on a particular project, I would try it, and if it failed, I'd just say "Oh, well" and move on to my next "fantasy."

Many of us will squander our last dollar and then rely on God to provide for us. God is a provider—there's no questioning that—but we are foolish and unrealistic if we expect him to support our unrealistic spending or foolish behavior. We have to be smarter than that; it is simply what God expects. Some of us think we will eventually get rich, and others think people owe them something. Some people rely on a slavery mentality; they think they have been oppressed and are now free but expect what has been taken from them will be returned.

If you were imprisoned and the warden told you, "Go! You're free; you've done your time," wouldn't you run as fast as you could and never look back? You would make the best of a free life and become the best you can. You will not want to relive your imprisonment; you will be looking to the future positively.

Why do some of us hold on to our imprisoned mentalities? That just subjects us to generational curses without end. We wonder why our grandparents, our brothers and sisters, hang on to their pasts, but we ourselves hang around the prison door eating, drinking, sleeping, living, giving birth, and thus cause generation after generation to relive the past.

When will we behave as children of Christ? "Ask, and it will be given to you; seek, and you will find; knock, and it will be opened to you" (Matthew 7:7). We have to recognize and acknowledge change, because once we pray and believe, change will come. A prayer isn't a monologue; it's a dialogue between us and God, so when we pray, he will respond. It may take years for that response, and we may be used to immediate responses—think of the fast Internet access we all expect—but we have to be as children who trust our nurturer. Babies cry at feeding time, but they know they will be fed. We may have headaches and heartaches, but our nurturer, God Almighty, hears us and will supply our needs. "And my God will meet all your needs according to the riches of his glory in Christ Jesus" (Philippians 4:19). I always trust his response will come even though at times it seems to take forever.

Lord, you've answered me many times and are still answering, so I know you work according to your will and not the will of man. "For a thousand years in your sight are but as yesterday when it is past, or as a watch in the night" (Psalm 90:4).

Note to self: It's not my *Swatch* or *Hello Kitty* watch but the master's clock that is involved here. How dare I think of

God as a simple magician; he is far greater than that, and if I allow our watches to become synchronized by praying and asking for wisdom, strength, and understanding in his time, not mine, I will learn he is always on time.

Help us, God, get out of the enemies' way of thinking about time, and help us dream big but according to your will. Help us to be rational and reasonable, allowing you to lead us through our short pilgrimage on earth. Give those of us with the desire to be rich the desire first to be rich spiritually so your Spirit may lead us. Help us not to be greedy. "For the love of money is a root of all kinds of evil. Some people, eager for money, have wandered from the faith and pierced themselves with many griefs" (1 Timothy 6:10).

Many of us are diverted by songs, movies, and other influences that associate richness with happiness. It is great to be financially prosperous, but money is meant to be used, and people are meant to be loved, so don't love money instead of people, and don't use people instead of money.

Money can make people do evil things, according to the Bible; money should not be more important than love, happiness, and life itself. How many rich people have committed suicide? Was that God's will? How many rich people are depressed and deprived of relationships with family, friends, and coworkers? Once riches go, so do relationships.

God knows us before we even know ourselves; he is the God who was, is, and will be. We must love God, and use our money for important things; that's the mind frame we need, eternal and genuine, in good and bad times.

My grandmother, Miss Babz—may God rest her soul—used to say to my cousins and me when we were about to do something stupid, "I didn't raise any fool." It's the same with our eternal Father, who says, "I didn't raise any fool." All God's children have to be wise with their financial blessings, use humility to lift others who are without, and give to others according to God's will, not our own understanding.

Those of us who are without should thank God for what we have and be wise, not singing a "sad sonky," a sad song, about what we lack but seek self-improvement. Where there's a will, there's a way. Go back to school; America offers many educational opportunities people elsewhere in the world would literally die for. The Internet allows us to educate ourselves. We should take Marcus Garvey's advice and read instead of spending hours watching TV, chatting on our cell phones, or idly browsing the Internet. When we get in the habit of reading, we will be better able to teach our children.

We must also read the Bible, which I consider to be a GPS that will lead us through life. I challenge you to give Bibles for Christmas presents rather than GPS units, and every time you use a navigation program on your cell phone, make up for that by reading a book of the Bible. Take the time to pray and to share God with others so his Word will be fruitful. "Then the way you live will always honor and please the Lord, and your lives will produce every kind of good fruit. All the while, you will grow as you learn to know God better and better" (Colossians 1:10).

No Small Change

We can't think in millions but work in pennies; we can't expect to achieve eternal faith through sitting and engaging in small talk—small change—and expect something of so much greater value to come. We can't allow the enemy to pin us down. We have to give 100 percent. We are Christians, right? Have you ever seen Christ function at less than 100 percent? Even at age twelve, Jesus went out to pray by himself, so age should be no barrier. Whether we are twelve or five times twelve, we have to tap into ourselves, stop living by what we see, by sight, and start living by faith of what is to come, what has been promised. We must strive for "betterment" by becoming better sons and daughters, fathers and mothers, workers, listeners, wives and husbands—better Christians. "The earth is the LORD's, and everything in it, the world, and all who live in it" (Psalm 24:1).

We as Christians can overcome our "imprisoned" mentalities. In accordance with God's will, we can achieve better spiritual, physical, emotional, and even financial positions with God's help.

I pray for faith and the strength to perform good works, because faith without works is a fantasy. I pray against this deep, dark fantasy that things will come to us without work, commitment, and oneness with God. I pray for God's direction to do as he pleases. I pray that God will bless us with the strength and desire to want to work and have faith, because we are often lazy on our own. I pray for all to be released from this way of thinking, this generational curse, in Jesus' name, amen.

The Bridge of the Song

I take pleasure in writing. I feel a divine peace and direction allowing me to write, and where this takes me I leave in the hands of the Lord. I guess this part in the book is the equivalent to the "bridge" of a song. I felt this calmness, and I thought I should be a writer. I am praying about this feeling, and I ask God to forgive me because I thanked him in doubt. *Me, Lord, Write?* I now realize that doubt is from the Devil, and I pray loudly, "I rebuke Satan in the name of Jesus."

Lord, I want to share with young people that if I had been in tune with you all these past years, I wouldn't have waited until my twenty-eighth year to realize your will for my life. All this time I have acted against you, I have sinned. Forgive me, Lord, and please give my family the strength to do your will. I want to say that I am looking for success, but that would be redundant, because doing your will is success. Sigh. Thank you, Lord Jesus.

Whenever we feel we're in control of things, we should be careful; that feeling is not a good sign. We need to be on a "stripped" level, a humbled level, so we will be led by God rather than ourselves.

At times, I think that my patients are doing well. Their IV lines are connected, and their situations are not as dire or demanding as they had been just a day or two earlier. That's when I stop and think I shouldn't be complacent about anything. One patient may be a preemie possibly facing cerebral palsy or blindness—the list of what can be a premature infant's prognosis is long. I realize I have much to do. I must realize that statistics come from man and that I, as a Christian, have to pray that by the grace of God—not statistics, not man—babies are healed.

Against All Odds

God defies all odds. LOL, you sports fans! Remember when he defied all odds and Tim Tebow and the Denver Broncos defeated the Pittsburgh Steelers? I pray you all were moved by that. On a more serious note, though, no matter what team we root for, we should be humbled by God's greatness; that's our best bet.

"He's Able" was a Sunday school song I used to sing; it tells us that God heals the brokenhearted, sets captives free, makes the lame walk, and causes the blind to see. He is a God able to fulfill all you entrust to him.

One time, when I was fasting, I realized that fasting without prayer is simply dieting; it may be healthy physically but not spiritually. I realized that when fasting, as Jesus did, I needed to be humbly yearning for God and hungry for his face and his answers. This should be the constant mental state of believers, who should not idolize certain foods or shun other foods during fasts, letting the food take precedence over prayer.

God told Peter that everything he made was clean. God told us in the Bible that it doesn't matter what goes into our mouths; what matters is what comes out of our mouths. We all need to look to him and pray for a continued desire for him, the truth, and the way.

Thank you, Lord, for this opportunity to fast, pray, and write. I hope it will be a blessing to many.

Many people, when they become rich, put basketball courts, tennis courts, or movie theaters in their houses. Why don't you ever hear about someone installing a chapel, a small, reverent place where family and visitors can pray and bow to the Most High? Such a space would be a significant, holy, and peaceful spot for talking to God and hearing his voice. If tennis fans can create tennis courts and basketball fans create basketball courts, then fans of God—of which I am one—can create praying "courts."

Help Us off Our High Horses, Lord

Hosanna forever! We worship you, Lord. Forgive me for not praying first thing in the morning, because we can sense your presence when we pray first thing. Help us to pray the last thing at night as well, because anything can happen in between, especially when we are on our high horses.

Christians aren't better than others, and you are above us all; we have to give you alone the honor and the glory. At times, we get on our high horses. I named my particular high horse "Naïve," and quite a few things happened in my life that have taken me down. I thank you, God, for your assistance in getting off that horse.

What's the name of your horse? This may be a good time to ask for God's assistance in getting off it. Whether it is pride, guilt, jealousy, confusion, disobedience, selfishness—whatever it is—come down from it before you are knocked down. I was knocked down from mine, and my chest plate surely burnt.

I want to acknowledge you, because I know by doing this, you will intervene and create understanding, wisdom, and strength in me. I will be humbled under your right hand, realizing that I need you in everything.

I love you, Lord, and I don't want to have this feeling of loving you solely because of the great things you are doing for me right now; I want to love you for the things to come and my past experiences that have shaped and strengthened me. Help me to trust in your direction and be knowledgeable of your desires, not mine. Help me get better spiritually, emotionally, and financially.

Take Your Stand

I enjoy Fred Hammond's "Just Stand," a song in which he relates how he took a stand and lost his best friend by doing that but wanted to live right rather than live in hell. Stand for holiness, stand for righteousness, and stand even if you lose friends.

Last year—I think ever since I became a Christian—I lost closeness with many people. My becoming a Christian shone a light on fewer similarities and more differences between them and me. I've let go of a lot because I didn't want to be a hypocrite in God's eyes. I can't go clubbing or partying if I want to endorse him. I can't hate people for what they have done to me; I have to pray for them. I still love my unsaved friends and those who have backslidden; I pray for their salvation.

I know many people who don't have close relationships with God; I was once like that. Some experience shame or embarrassment when they decide to become Christians, but that is the work of the enemy; he opposes the goodness God has in store for us. I appreciate the boldness God has given me to take a stand for him.

Dear Lord, at times, I think of where to look for you, where to pray to or praise you. I find myself staring into dark cabinets at work but imagining that I am looking at the sky, where I believe you are. However, I've grown to realize that's not true. You're in the bedroom with us, on the school bus with us, at work with us, at the bedside of the patients we take care of, in the kitchen with us, in the trucks we drive, and in school with our kids. Wherever we are, you are right there; you are an everywhere God. We often tend to ignore your presence, but it's only because of your love and passion that we exist.

Forgive Us Our Sins, Lord

Forgive us, God, because if we just pray more, you will burst through and infiltrate the minds of homosexuals, adulterers, fornicators, and all of us who sin against your Word. "You shall not lie with a male as with a woman; it is an abomination" (Leviticus 18:22); "You shall not commit adultery" (Exodus 20:14). The Bible mentions lust as a form of adultery, so we really have to check ourselves. How many of us have had or are having sex outside marriage? According to the Bible, this is fornication, which defiles our bodies.

Sexual abuse of children is a sin against God; "It would be better for him if a milestone were hung around his neck and he were thrown into the sea than for him to cause one of these little ones to sin" (Luke 17:2). Though it is such a sin to harm God's children, many people fall short and inflict hurt upon them.

We should beg for forgiveness because we have all sinned. Sins are sins, whether natural or unnatural, whether they are not that serious (a white lie) or are extremely odious (murder). Get a mixing bowl and throw them all in, because they are all sins. Every time you lie, every time a child is sexually abused, every time someone is murdered, every time a man lies with a man, or a woman with a woman, or a human with an animal, it is a slap in God's face. These things are forces of darkness, spirits we have no control over unless we seek God's face.

We may want to sin because it feels good, or tell a lie to get out of or into a situation, but we must realize that if we don't get penalized about it ourselves, our next of kin, the next generation will.

If we had taken all the slaps God has taken, our faces would be red and our eyes full of fury. However, if we turn away from these ways, he will forgive us. God does not hate the sinner; he hates the sin, according to his Word.

None of us can point fingers, as none of us is perfect. "How can you say to your brother, 'Brother, let me take the speck out of your eye,' when you yourself fail to see the plank in your own eye? You hypocrite, first take the plank out of your eye, and then you will see clearly to remove the speck from your brother's eye" (Luke 6:42).

Look at it this way: we are all siblings, and our father has left us at home but will return shortly. He left us some rules, as parents always do, and we had better keep them until he gets back; none of us wants to be guilty of anything when he gets back. We have to look at ourselves as children and at God as our father. We can't bash each other; we have to encourage each other to live as our father wants us to.

How hypocritical of us to hate homosexuals but not adulterers. Let us get those logs out of our eyes before we complain about others' specks. If we ever think we are faultless, we should ask God about that; he will point out our faults. We must all be honest with ourselves and ask God for forgiveness for all these moments we've slapped him in the face. God is the master of time, of everything. Let us repent now, not next year, not even tomorrow, because the next five minutes are not a certainty. We must ask for forgiveness and live a healthy and conscious life through God's will.

Getting to Heaven

The Bible tells us how we can get to heaven. I couldn't grasp this concept at first because I thought everybody got to heaven. We talk about people looking down from heaven, but how do we know they are really there? Did they truly accept and love God as the Bible tells us to? I think back on loved ones I have lost, and I have to wonder when I wished that they would rest in peace if it would be so or if their souls would be eternally restless.

Where will you or I go when we leave earth? At times, none of us is worthy to see God's face because we preach one thing but do another. God's Word says many things, such as "Thou shall not kill" (Exodus 20:13), that we ignore through laws that allow abortion and neighborhoods where murder is commonplace. God Almighty is against homosexuality, but many people consider homosexuality a simple act of self-expression, and certain states now allow same-sex marriages. We are tolerant of this, but we should understand why God destroyed Sodom and Gomorrah. He deemed no one worthy among them.

I wish there would be a people who would preach and practice your word, O Lord, but we all fall short. Unless people are called out about their sins or are prayed for, they can be in such a depth of darkness that they don't realize what they are doing or that they are being controlled by the master of sins himself, the Devil.

We are in big trouble! I feel that too many people are too comfortable with their lifestyles and behaviors. It's as if they have given up their homes and want to live on the beach, on vacation, all the time. People are complacent on earth because heaven seems so far away. I know that when I go to the Caribbean for a vacation, I'm tempted to stay forever and not go home to New York. People love this world, so they ask, "Heaven who? Heaven what?" They forget we are just passing through life; it's just a short vacation itself. "Dear friends, I warn you as 'temporary residents and foreigners' to keep away from worldly desires that wage war against your very souls" (1 Peter 2:11).

We become the things of the world instead of impacting the world. It's as if we visit Mexico and suddenly start trying to speak the language and wearing sombreros to fit in. We live in such contentment that we don't expect anything out of the norm to happen, let alone the return of Christ. "For as the lightning comes from the east and flashes to the west, so will be the coming of the Son of man" (Matthew 24:27).

People are deceived that homosexuality is okay through lack of enlightenment; some think that child abuse is okay if no one finds out about it, and some women cover their scars after being battered, thinking that will make everything okay.

News flash—after night comes day, right? Darkness leaves when light comes. The same way we desire to buy that pair of shoes we saw or that new car we want is the same way God desires to come back for the just in this world. If we humans can go to great extremes to satisfy our hearts' desires, let us go to the same extremes to realize that God is coming back.

Think of your life—your past and your present. Unless they are "squeaky" clean according to the will of God, and Christlike, you may not be going to heaven. Be aware of this possibility and pray for the now, what's to come, and to overcome generational curses.

As innocent as many of us might be, our family histories linger with sins that fall on us or our children. Let us pray and fast that God will cause a supernatural breakthrough, heal us, and give us all clean slates to free us of our pasts. We must pray for forgiveness for our ancestors, because many of them might have not, and that's the reason we carry their sins.

Even though you have sinned, pray for forgiveness, because God hears and forgives hearts that believe in him, trust him, and sincerely want his forgiveness. The Devil will lie to you; he will put in your head that you did a bad thing and may continually remind you of it or the wrongs you have suffered at others' hands. This is not good; it's simply reliving the past rather than trusting God for forgiveness, which will renew you.

Living in this past can also let those who have wronged us feel unforgiven, and they could live in misery, feeling scarred for life. Who are we to inflict such misery, no matter what has been done to us? Even Jesus forgave the men who crucified him. Have you ever been crucified, nailed to a cross? No. Did any of your wounds ever come close to this? Not even. Do people do things to you that words can't explain? Yes, so forgive and forget. No one is perfect, and if we want forgiveness, we have to forgive others; we cannot manipulate those who hurt us by bringing up the past—we have to move on.

The Wages of Sin

All sins, small and large, are acts against God; whether you bake, boil, or steam that mixing bowl in which they are, the end product is death. "For the wages of sins is death, BUT the free gift of God is eternal life in Christ Jesus our Lord" (Romans 6:23). We all have committed sins, sexual sins with the opposite or the same sex, or lying on a small scale or a grand-jury-type scale; we all have dipped in that mixing bowl, and we all need forgiveness.

We humans categorize sins on our own terms: adultery is a greater sin than stealing a piece of candy, or being in a "committed" boyfriend-and-girlfriend relationship is different from fornication, but all sin is a slap in God's face.

We have to realize we were born in sin, so everything is of sin, unless we make the choice to get out of sin and its consequences, death, by seeking God and following his Word.

Please note well that according to the Bible, we can get to know God for free. Anybody jumping or getting excited about that? I bet the majority is not. Anyone for free breakfast in the staff lounge? Anyone for free dinner for a family of four at a local eatery? Many would surely jump on those offers, just as they gravitate toward signs that read, "Buy one, get one free."

Eternal life is free, but in many cases, it's the least of our concerns. Do we understand how twisted our priorities are? How diverted from the will of God we are? The truth is available, and salvation is free. God "desires all people to be saved and to come to the knowledge of the truth" (1 Timothy 2:4). Ours is a forgiving God; no matter what we've done, whatever sins we have contributed to that mixing bowl of sins, we can be forgiven. The Devil condemns, implanting in us obsessive, insane thoughts, but God doesn't.

Protection from Satan's Arrows and Hell

Seeking God is easier said than done. We may want to abide in God, but the Devil, the master of sin, will torment us with his arrows that pierce our hearts. If, however, we are mindful, prayerful, and in the will of God, he will offer us protection from those arrows and the flames of hell.

Christians and non-Christians alike can paint a picture in their heads of a place populated with trillions of people who are burning forever. Their agony is never ending and unendurable. They want to get out but never will. Sounds like hell, right? It is! And I'm sure it's a "zillion" times worse than my description.

A childhood friend of mine was baptized; she became a Christian. As a teenager, I thought she must have been crazy to have become a Christian; I thought she didn't realize what she'd be missing. I wondered how she could leave all the sinful things we used to do to become a Christian. She, however, shared with me something that made her decide to give her life to Jesus, something that has stuck with me ever since. She told me how one night she had dreamed she was in hell. She told me of the fire and the agony and how that had convinced her she didn't want to end up in hell.

The scene she had painted in my mind replayed like a Michael Jackson video, over and over. The more I watched it, the more I realized I needed to "beat it," to get rid of the junk and hindrances in my life, dispel my unrealistic understandings of what being a Christian meant, and just let go and let God.

If you aren't in a maximal relationship with God, the time is now. Nothing wishy-washy—you have to dive in for the "kill," that is, get rid of what you think might be the shame of becoming a Christian, let go of bad habits, and put an end to negative relationships or influences that hinder your chance of gaining eternal life. You must be mindful that the Lord says, "Whoever is not with me is against me, and whoever does not gather with me scatters" (Matthew 12:30).

Questions for All of Us

Are you composed by God's grace? Do you have an unexplainable peace? Do you have a spiritual instinct of what's right and wrong? Do you remain prayerful? Do you understand that fearing God does not mean being physically or spiritually afraid of him or thinking he's unapproachable? Do you understand he is above us all, and he has to be honored, respected, trusted, and appreciated as number one in your life?

Does your lifestyle preclude your having a conversation with God? Are your acts better off behind closed doors than in the light? Are you confused about life? Are you often depressed? Are you manipulative and deceitful? Do you inflict pain on others?

This list of questions could go on because we have all fallen short, but now is a great time to explore and guarantee yourself eternal life. Let go of history and be embraced and delighted by the amazement of God.

Help Us, Lord

Whenever I'm feeling tired or my husband or family is feeling sick, I pray earnestly, help us, Lord; help us so that sickness won't take up the time we need to dedicate to you or your work. Don't let doubt or confusion in, but help us to pray continually and be healthy, godly individuals.

Thank you for the strength to care for people in our lives. As your agents, we want to embody such Christian characteristics that people will search deeper to know our drive and want the same thing that drives us, which is you, Lord. We thank you.

Dear God, I haven't dedicated everything you have given me to your work. You give me faith, but I settle for just fearing the enemy. You clearly put in my spirit my care group, I Love My Sister, but I fear it will be a failure. Dear God, part of me knows it is flourishing and I just have to fulfill your will, but I feel weary at times, fearing no one will attend our meetings, and I feel that I'll be judged even if people do show up. But God, if you're going to use me, I have to be fully available. I may fail man on earth, but glory prevails in heaven.

I think about how, before I was saved, I listened to pastors, speakers, and others giving messages about God. Little by little, sermon after sermon, I have held on to my faith up to this day, and it has changed my life.

Lord, I pray that everyone in the world, especially the young women of I Love My Sister and those who are reading this book, finds love, peace, forgiveness, prosperity, and goodness, and by that I mean Christ Jesus. You are God, the beginning and the end, and until anyone has developed a relationship with you, he or she is "dead."

Help me because I'm weary at times, and fasting makes me hungry. My belly is growling, and I feel my body changing. Forgive me for not praying as much as I want to, but please let me be so close to you that I can hear your heartbeat, just as children held tightly by their mothers can hear their heartbeats. I love you and thank you for everything.

Dear God, there is evil around us. We rush and think of worldly things. Your kingdom is far from our thoughts for most of our lives. Unless we become sick and fall flat on our faces, we think about you briefly and then move on to our next thoughts. We are swimming at sea; we can't control our bodies, and our minds are not our own—we lie down, we dream; we wake up, we still dream. We are not ourselves; we, your children, become chameleons by blending in to the things of this world. The world desires to overtake and partake in us, and we desire to overtake and partake in the things of the world. How sweet you are, how glorious you are, for forgiving us when we act against you.

Forgive us, Lord, because we have sinned. I know you're a forgiving God. You forgive us for times we glorify man instead of glorifying you, your mercies, and your favors. You love us the same way I love my children; I don't let even a fly touch them even when they're in the wrong. I know, O God, you let us learn from our wrongs, just as I teach my son by rewards and reprimands. You snatch us from the enemy and nurture us to grow and be better for you; you know what's best for us.

You created us, and we belong to you. We don't belong anywhere else; we'd be like monkeys being raised by lions. We humans can't teach monkeys to be monkeys, and cats can't teach rats to be rats, so how can any other force—the Devil, the world—teach us to be like God, to be peaceful, prosperous, and enjoy abundant, guiltless lives?

Mold us, God; direct us to be more like you, because even though you created us in your image, we are far from being your protégés. We love you, Lord, and we thank you for awakening our brains and giving us spiritual CPR no matter how far we drift from you. Thank you for the constant opportunities you give us to submit to you so you can teach us to be less selfish and more like you, a devoted, up-and-beyond God, and not to wait until the drum rolls and your kingdom comes.

Foolish Thoughts

I, for one, used to think very foolishly. I thought I could live my life as I wanted, and on the day when the clouds opened, I could run to the closest church, get baptized, and get into heaven. Surprisingly, many people think unrealistically, out of tune with God. I know I did until I was saved.

I vividly remember a comment a customer made to me one day when I was working at a pharmacy. Someone was preaching about God to those waiting in line to pick up their medicine, and a young man, about twenty-five, responded in a rebellious Jamaican accent, "From mi lickle and ah grow God ah come, and God still can't come yet." He was saying that since he was a child, he had been hearing that God would come soon, but he was an adult then, and God had not yet returned. A young man with no reverence for God's promise to return! It was a sad encounter, and I pray for that young man; I can still remember his face.

God, your Word says you will appear like a thief in the night, that no one will know the hour or the minute of your return. We may grow weary, and some of us will revert to our own ways and understanding. Wake us, Lord; let us stay abreast with you in all our ways and thoughts and know that you will return to save us, not destroy us. We want to be ready when you return. Allow us to be ready, Lord, and not fall off this narrow road.

As I sit in the bathroom writing this, with my son messing with the towels, I don't know how many eyes will read this, but I pray that your blood, Lord, will prepare them despite their pasts, current circumstances, and lack of faith in their futures. Prepare their hearts, souls, and spirits for your return, in Jesus' name, amen.

The Devil's "Blessings"?

I was praying in a chapel at work during my breakfast break. When the pastor started talking about witchcraft, it dawned on me how evil people can be. People feed into evil, and the Devil influences people to do and say evil things. I guess that's what the pastor meant when he said that the Devil can "bless" people too. Yes, the Devil can anchor untruths in people's hearts and minds and cause them to do evil things.

Lord, by the blood of Jesus, I pray your protection upon my family. "Do not hide your face from me, do not turn your servant away in anger; you have been my helper, do not reject me or forsake me God my Savior" (Psalm 27:9). The enemy seeks our destruction, so we beg your deliverance. Thank you, Jesus.

I also recall the pastor talking about how we Christians need renewal time after time, which made perfect sense to me. Just as married couples renew their vows, we Christians need to get back to basics and reexperience that desperate need for God's forgiveness. We can't allow things to get dry and outdated. God is a living God, and our faith has to be living as well with constant refreshers, renewal, commitment, and communication with God.

I thank God for a continued opportunity to fast. I feel the Devil intruding, causing me fear, and wanting me to believe I'm hearing things. Once, when I was eating fish, I almost thought the fish skin was a snake's skin, the skin of the enemy. Because the Devil is a liar, we must pray constantly for protection, deliverance, favor, and mercy, or we will end up in big trouble.

The Devil shows up especially when glory is going to God, when breakthroughs are occurring, when people are seeking God. I rebuke the Devil in Jesus' name, and I pray for the strength to keep a tight grip on the Lord. I lay down all areas of my life to him for protection. "Ask and it shall be given to you. Seek and ye shall find. Knock and it shall be opened unto you" (Matthew 7:7).

I believe in your Word, Lord, and I am knocking on heaven's door for your angels to hover over this nation and for the Holy Spirit to draw people so close to you that they will submit their lives to you, in Jesus' name. I'm waiting, Lord, and I trust in you that it is already done, amen.

In Your Presence Always, **Lord**

Thank you, Lord, for the sun in the day and the moon at night; you made everything, and we rejoice in it. I want to be in your presence always. One morning, I was thinking about my future, about how I wanted to become an actress living in a pleasant neighborhood and sharing your goodness with young women. I know the enemy will force desires on us for his sake, but, dear Lord, I pray that your vision for us will be crystal clear, so help us to be obedient and sensitive to it.

I know that the enemy's desires will seem at times more favorable, worldly, and easier to accomplish, but give us the strength that whether your plans for us are easy or hard, we will have the desire to fulfill them. Forgive us our sins, and make us better people, better Christians. Help us to need you always; help us not to run to you just at unfavorable times but at all times. You're not a God of "badness" who sends "signs" or punishments.

Lord, I always tell the women of I Love My Sister to never stop praying; when things are great, that's when they should pray even more, because when things get rough, their stored-up prayers will carry them through. Help us to be so close to you that we can clearly hear your voice. You alone are God, and you deserve honor, glory, and praise. You are an "everytime" and "everything" God, and you want continual and absolute relationships with us.

Believing in God's Promises

Dear Lord, forgive me, because as I think about my disobedience in the past, I see how silly I have been. One night, I heard that a snowstorm was coming the next morning, but I ignored the prediction. I heard you remind me to leave my windshield wipers in the up position, but no one else was taking that precaution, so I just walked in my house and totally disobeyed you. I learned quite a few lessons from this: I should be obedient, I shouldn't follow what other people are doing, and the meteorologist was not joking when he said there would be a snowstorm.

We believe what we see, not what is promised. We have a "here and now" way of thinking. If we don't see it, we don't have faith in it. We are so self-reliant that it's almost as if we want to answer our own prayers and strengthen ourselves. We have to obey, act on things not yet seen, and believe that if it has been promised, it will come about. Unless we're prepared, we will lose out on God's grace and blessings.

Putting On Our Shows

My work with premature babies involves infants from birth to five months old. Some of our team members gush over babies when parents are present, but when the parents leave, it's a different ball game; that supposed passion for the infants disappears. One staff member, who was not a nurse, was so into one baby, playing and talking with the infant, but only when she noticed the mother coming over. My thought was, *Really? I haven't seen her with that attitude toward the baby when the parents aren't around.* It was an act to make Mom believe she was always like that with her child.

Isn't that like us all? We always put on a show; we think that when people are around, we should act one way, and when no one is around, we think we don't have to account for our actions. A single person could justify being in several intimate relationships by thinking, *Nothing's wrong with this because I'm not married.* Someone could justify spending money behind a spouse's back in the same way.

The greatest gift you can give yourself is being yourself; it's so much easier than trying to be someone else. Many of us don't know where our future leads because we are living someone else's life. We should pay attention to our truths no matter who is watching—and trust me, someone is always watching. By doing this, we will be able to realize things in our lives that are stifling us.

Thank you, Father, for everything. Thank you for insight, the ability to understand things that at first don't make sense to us. Your will stands, and we have to lean on your understanding, not our own.

After listening to a sermon about forgiveness, I remembered how I had treated someone who had passed away; the memory weighed on me. Let us not let malice rule our lives. I have never heard a dead person talk back. You will be able to apologize to someone at his or her funeral, but you will not get his or her forgiveness; you will simply regret what could've been. Be aware of the high horse you are on, of your attitude that you don't need someone, so you won't be tormented by the could haves and should haves.

Thy Will Be Done

Good morning, sweet Jesus, our Savior. One weekend, I invited people to a little birthday party for my son. I prayed that the ones you wanted to be there would come, but I can count the people who came on one hand. I felt angry and disappointed; I felt as though my "enemy" button had been activated. Then I recalled that I had asked for your will to be done, and I realized that some of the people I had invited who hadn't come were not in your will. I ask forgiveness for my anger and allowing my emotions to control me; I'm so glad I didn't post something disrespectful on Facebook.

I thank you, because we had a terrific time. Thank you for those people who weren't there; you were there, and according to your Word, you will always be there.

I know, dear God, that sometimes you teach us how to do without certain people or things. We ask you to show up, and when you do, we get angry or disappointed in the things you show up for. Help us appreciate your will and our situation, and help us to trust your work and not get angry at people for what they do or don't do to us or for us. Help us to be humbled by our experiences and grow from them.

I thank you for the opportunity to vent and pray for the strength to continue to witness through writing. I am humbled by this platform to tell how great you are, hallelujah! You have given me this medium. Dear God, I feel very weary at times, but I pray for breakthroughs, favors, and to be financially savvy.

Waking Up from a Deep Sleep

How can we work our way to Christ after we have walked away or if we were never with him at all? Pastor Jentezen Franklin shares on his website and in his book how the enemy has put us in deep sleep. I know it's true; I remember that when I was growing up, I was living in a dream, having moments when I would tap back into reality. I was not in contact with God; I felt the need to always doze off deep into thoughts. I was living under the influence of the enemy; it was as if I were drunk, doing things I would not have done sober. I grew up feeling lost and wanting to be found. I lived, but I was sleeping; my spirit was dead.

I was set free, however. I woke up to the point that I can look at my past and see things I never was able to see before. I'm not perfect, and I still have flaws, but I compare it to this: We all have felt that weird, tingling sensation when our feet or our hands have "fallen asleep" and start "waking up." Well, we're sleeping on God's will, God's treasure. We all have to ask, "God, please come into my life, be with me and rescue me from this deep sleep so I won't be numb to my purpose in life, numb to family and friends, but to be alive and well, to be happy, and to sense your presence in the not-so-fortunate times."

Dear God, I have had some heartbreaking moments in my life. I call them *moments* now, but when I was going through them, they seemed to be years. To you, God, they are short, and we can grow in faith through these experiences. With you, God, there is a sense of assurance, a peace that surpasses all understanding. I can't believe I'm saying this! I used to raise my eyebrow when people said that, but now I understand it. If you don't, you're not in your place with Christ, a place of entirety and oneness with him. You can, however, achieve this peace.

I tell those who are afraid of taking the test to get a driver's license not to be worried; I say that if I can get a license, they can as well. (My husband will second that.) In the same way, nothing is too big or too small for God; he is the King of Kings who gave me, a crazy girl, his abiding peace, and he will give it to you as well if you trust him.

Don't act on your own; don't let others pressure you—tap deeper for what God wants you to do. In this way, you will have no regret, depression, or anger. You will be able to survive and let go of hail, snow, fires, breakups—any and all of life's storms. Trust God to deliver you from the past, present, and future.

God Is Always "In"

I sometimes went on depressive rants about things such as my hair. One time, after I got my hair braided, I decided that it was really not the "in" thing and that I needed something more economical and easier to maintain. I felt that I wouldn't be accepted; I was worried about pleasing others, about following the crowd. I asked God to help me decide what to do with my hair. You see the things we have to involve Christ in and acknowledge him? It's great when we allow him in and ask him what to wear or how to comb our hair, because these things do matter, as we have to be in sync with his vision for us.

However, the thing with me (and I'm sure with you as well) is that I ask questions but don't listen for answers. I beg for his forgiveness. I'd rushed to get my braids without his answer. I was envisioning something great, mind you; I appreciate hair braiders for their time and effort, but that one time, I disliked the result; it just didn't do anything for me, and that was my mother's opinion as well.

I went back to the hairdresser with a prayer and the hope she could change it to a Mohawk style, something with more hair out, or ultimately just pull out my braids. However, she wouldn't change it or even give me my money back; it was late in the day, and she needed to get home to feed her children. She told me that I had asked for braids and had gotten them. I felt so hurt, sad, stupid, and foolish. I had spent $100; this is the part where I did some "cow bawling," crying very loud. I could have used the money to pay down my student loan; I pray in the name of Jesus that she put the $100 to good use for her children.

I must confess, nonetheless, that I felt so relieved and privileged to speak to God about this; I asked for forgiveness for not allowing his Holy Spirit to lead me.

I beg for you to rescue me, Lord, because the enemy has intervened in my happiness, and I pray to continue with you no matter what challenges come my way. Lord, I understand that certain things won't always be normal or "in," but you are a God who is always "in." Let us hold on to you and be grateful, mindful, and thankful to you always. I realize now that if it takes stepping out of the box, the "in," to be happy, as the pastor who visited my church shared, why spend money we don't have on things we don't need to please people we don't like?

I love you, Lord, and I thank you for loving us no matter how spoiled and foolish we can be at times. Let your peace, grace, and happiness be upon us all, in Jesus' name, amen.

Thank you, God, for your continued concern for us, an ungrateful people. The enemy makes us forget to give you the glory, the thanks, and the praise you deserve. Glory belongs to you, God, and the battle is not ours—it's yours. I thank you on behalf of my family, my friends, my coworkers, my neighbors, the people I come across, the people who come across me, the people reading this book, and everyone else.

Dear God, I thought of my mom while in the shower last night and how, whether I want to hear the truth or not, she always tells it. If something is not right, if it "ain't popping," whether hair, clothes, conversations, attitudes, she lets me know straight up, and I admire her boldness. Although the truth is hard to digest at times, you don't hide things either, Master. Your light exposes the truth that sets us free. We can run and hide, but the truth is visible at all times. We thank you for the peace we get with your truth.

Whether it's a bad-hair day or our attitude, God puts us in check. Anything that is not the truth is a lie, a work of the enemy's, who is always trying to tap into our thoughts and manipulate us to see and think things that are not true. The enemy can try to use our flaws to get rid of our will and purpose in God.

Help Me Conquer My Insecurities, Lord

I remember being so insecure in my relationship with my husband, even to the point of worrying about not being a great cook. My insecurities would lead me to have jealous thoughts when he would have lengthy conversations with others, even my own friends. I would indulge in thoughts that he likes her and would break up with me for her or anyone else who could cook. Those were dark and depressive thoughts prompted by the enemy, who knew I was in an insecure place.

I dare him, however, to try me now that I've become so close to God that I can touch him and hear his every word. I love my husband dearly, and I trust him, adore him, and appreciate the man he has become. We've known each other since high school, and here we are, years older and still together because of God's grace and mercy, for which I am thankful.

Thank you, Lord, for giving me the courage to learn how to cook; I realize that when we draw close to you, our flaws decrease, and the enemy flees. "Submit yourselves, then, to God. Resist the Devil, and he will flee from you" (James 4: 7). We thank you for your Word.

Lord, I know you gather with us in our I Love My Sister meetings so we can help others better themselves. We can show others that you are real, that there is no course to take, no test to pass in getting to you. Our clothes do not matter, nor do our accents, our jobs, where we live, nor what we do or don't have as long as we pray and draw closer to you; that will free us of our insecurities. We had six beautiful young women at a previous setting; five attended the meeting before that, so we are definitely growing, but I pray many more will experience your peace

I must confess that before one meeting, I felt so insecure that I had the urge to cancel it; none of the twenty young women I invited had responded to my Facebook message. I was busy preparing for the meeting but still felt discouraged. Even leading up to the day I thought no one would come, but I am so glad you are close to me, and I followed through.

I trust in your Word, Lord, that says we should walk by faith, not by sight. Thanks to you, God, the meeting was a success, and I pray that all the women who attended will give their lives to you. Save them and their families, in Jesus' name, amen.

I pray against sickness, hurt, and depression, and I pray for health, peace, joy, and happiness for all who will attend I Love My Sister, and I pray for the millions who will read this book, in Jesus' name, amen.

Let Us Fulfill Your Purposes, Lord

I thank you, Lord, for the opportunity to go to church. Pastor Martha preached about Elijah, an ordinary man in an extraordinary time. She spoke about how you are always looking for ordinary people to do your work and to fulfill your purposes. I pray you give me the strength and understanding to fulfill my purpose for your kingdom.

It's funny how the more humbled I become, the emptier of self and pride, the more I understand life. How can you fill a wine container when it's full? When I was full of myself and felt super, conceited, naïve, and holier than anyone else, I was actually as hollow as can be. There wasn't any substance to my life; I had much but wanted more, I loved but I also hated, I was happy but I cried, and I ate but was still hungry. I'm glad you humbled me, Lord; I'm glad you cleaned out the bitter and useless wine and gave me the wine of your salvation. Hooray for Christ!

Lord, we frequently go down a list of things we want—vacations, bigger houses, new cars—without asking you about them and hearing from you first. "Therefore do not worry about tomorrow, for tomorrow will worry about itself. Each day has enough trouble of its own" (Matthew 6:34).

Let us pray and plan by saying "God's will" before anything we plan or do or hope for; that way, we will know and trust that if it is the Lord's will, it will be done. If it is not God's will, let us not get weary in spirit, because God sees and knows best. Let us be in that place where we can ultimately seek God, the ultimate counselor, the greatest financial advisor. He sits high and looks low, so when we can't see and understand things around us, he can offer us a master view.

Help us to be mindful of you, Lord, in our dreams and plans, praying your will be done, otherwise we labor in vain. "Unless the Lord builds the house, they labor in vain that build it: except the Lord keep the city, the watchman waketh but in vain" (Psalm 127:1).

All in God's Time

I have fasted and prayed for millions of things, and some of us have fasted and prayed for millions of dollars. I know, dear Lord, it is not in our time but in your time that we receive. You healed Lazarus in your time, not his sister's. Help us hold on until you do something.

When I was baptized, I prayed for my husband to be baptized right there and then, and I'm still praying and waiting for that. I prayed that he would own a truck route in May one year, and by July, he had purchased one, and not long after that, he bought an additional route. I thank God for answering our prayers, and I ask him to help us dedicate all we have and own, even our lives, to him.

You are a God of your Word, Lord; you said, "Ask, and it shall be given." I have learned that we pray for things subconsciously, expecting the thing or person we pray for will come all on its own. I have learned, however, that a drug addict can't stop being a drug addict, a person can't just will himself or herself to become a Christian, a liar can't stop lying—these changes require God.

We can't depend on our husbands to save themselves; only God saves, so we have to trust him to do so. Only God can let a person stop drinking; only God can cause a person to be honest; liars will tell lies until God blesses them with the truth. We have no authority without God—unless God, then nothing; it's as simple as that.

Our Idols

I recall a pastor preaching about "idolizing" things such as our families, sports, clothes, and so forth. I have to confess how I was once obsessed with Beyoncé and her daughter. I thought their story was entertaining, and I just couldn't get enough of it, but it was taking up all my free time. I would google her at lunchtime, and I would dream about her and her family. Nobody could say anything bad about Beyoncé. I idolized the way she dressed and the way she performed. Like her movie, I was "obsessed."

I had to get a grip on myself, to stop that fanatic type of behavior, and I am very glad I did. I love Beyoncé as a human being, not as a god, not as an idol, which my emotions had made her out to be. It had taken away from my time of worship with God.

We see a pair of shoes, idolize them, and spend our last dollars to get them. We can even idolize food; I had to give up chocolate one Lent because not only was it getting the best of my soul but also the best of my shape. The only thing we should crave, the only thing we cannot do without, is God, and we should seek his forgiveness if we ever let anything take his place.

I Pray for 20/20 Relationship Vision

I think about what agony young women have to go through to maintain their relationships with their children's fathers and their boyfriends, and I wonder why they do this. Why do women allow themselves to undergo pain over and over, the cheating, their men having babies with other women? These women are beautiful, motivated, and positive, and when I hear how deeply they want their relationships to work, my heart aches for them. It's not God's will that these women ache and moan.

If they would only listen to your voice, Lord. If they would just set a time every day to pray for direction in their relationships, maybe they would get 20/20 relationship vision and not be blindsided by these men and the constant heartaches they bring.

Sometimes a woman thinks she knows who the guy is for her; she may have a child by him and think theirs is the perfect family, but it's a false family, one she is forcing. That's not what God wants for her; she'll live in misery until she seeks and hears from him and obeys him.

Have you ever held dry sand? You squeeze it to keep it in your hands, but it shivers out of your grip and seeps out.

Most young women try to hold on to the impossible, but in due season it disappears, and the relationship is no more. I pray such young women will seek your face, Lord, for advice and strength in everything, especially their relationships, which should be on their front burners. I also pray that their men stop buying the milk and invest in the cow. I pray that as people we can stop fornicating by realizing it's a sin, an act against you, in Jesus' name, amen.

You Answer Our Prayers, Lord

I know it's not an "if" but a "when" when it comes to your answering our prayers, Lord. Your Word says that when we fast and pray, things will happen—bondages will be broken, yokes will be destroyed, demonic holds will be replaced with angelic holds, and good will conquer evil. I know you hear my pleas, and I wish I prayed more. I feel you, Lord, and I trust and know in my spirit you are with us all. Help us to be keen to your voice and obedient to your directions, the only way we will achieve lives of peace and abundance.

I pray for firstborns, your firstfruits. I dedicated my first, a son, to you. I pray that our firstborns, all our children, may be blessings to society. There are many wombs that need to be blessed, Lord. Please bless them and heal them so they will be fruitful.

I pray for our parents and the prayers they have bestowed upon us. I pray your greatness and goodness upon them. I pray this will be everyone's best year yet. You are the best in everything, so help us draw nearer to you, Lord. I feel so blessed and honored to have developed this closer relationship with you, and I know many reading this book have done or will do the same.

I love you, Lord, and I commit myself totally to you. I pray your health and strength descend upon all the premature, sickly babies I work with, and I pray for their parents, guardians, and households they will go home to. I pray that you will be with them, in Jesus' name.

I pray your will be done with my coworkers. Heal all the division, confusion, hurt, and malice, and let all work areas improve in every sense of the word, according to your will, in Jesus' name, amen. Thank you, Jesus, and breathe upon us, Holy Spirit. Hallelujah, in Jesus' name.

I can recall one time when I completed a fast and thought I could have used an "after fast." You know, when there's a party, there's an "after party"; well, we need an "after fast." I pray that all our after fasts may take the forms of steadfast commitment to God and be times of spiritual growth, activity, and conversation with God.

Deliver Us, O Lord

I pray against bad memories and years of doubt and shame. We grow up with so many unfavorable ties and associations. I remember being sexually abused at age seven. I was dumbfounded by it. I couldn't tell anyone about it; the guilt, shame, and embarrassment made me feel that a heavyweight boxer had punched me in the stomach. I couldn't talk or breathe. The Devil repeatedly tormented me with horrific memories of it, and I ended up trusting nothing, no one, not even myself. For years, it killed me softly.

I remember that in the beginning years of my marriage, when my husband would touch me, I would subconsciously cringe; I associated his touch with that of my abuser. It wasn't a good feeling for me, and it was very unfair to associate my husband with the abuse I had suffered.

I also remember that after I was abused, I was so rebellious, calling out for help, but abusers tell the abused not to say anything, and the abused can be so scared that they don't tell anyone. I wish I had spoken about it sooner; that would have saved me many unfavorable life events. I encourage all victims of abuse, no matter their age, to speak out. It was just a few years ago that I told my mom and my husband. I did not want to say anything earlier because I didn't want anyone to deem me condemned or abnormal, and I didn't want to be felt sorry for, which would have saddened my mom. I now know, however, that telling someone about abuse, past or present, can bring great relief.

Parents, if you notice rebellious behavior or something not right with your child or children, male or female, ask them what's going on; I guarantee that their rebellion is a cry for help. It may not be abuse, but it is a cry for help with something. Many of us have had dreadful thing happen to us, and the daily torment of the memory can swamp our ability to trust and our sanity. I questioned why certain things happened to me, and I have come to the understanding that humans do not operate themselves but are subject to bad or good influences. What some people have done to others is ugly and bad. The enemy seeks to devour and destroy; that's his job, so he is good at it, and he thinks he will have the last laugh, but his days are numbered.

I forgive the person the Devil used to rob me of many things. We abuse victims will have victory in Jesus, because everything taken from us mentally, physically, or spiritually will come back threefold, in Jesus' name, amen. We must let go of the past and live each day fresh, just as God's love is new for us each day. "Great is his faithfulness: his mercies begin afresh each morning" (Lamentations 3: 23).

Since I've been saved, I thought of quite a few things. For example, a guy might not let people know he's dating a particular girl, but she might be bragging about their dating; as well, a girl might not let people know she's dating a particular guy, but he's always talking about it; their feelings just aren't mutual. This scenario can occur with Christians—some people can be quiet about being Christians, but I want no mistake about it; I'm with God, Jesus Christ, and the Holy Spirit, and yes, the feeling is mutual.

We Belong in Heaven

I had a vision once of a woman burning in a fire. Her face was black, and she was bellowing in pain. Even though she was burned to the bone, she was still alive. I always joke with my cousins about refusing to go to hell. During the summer, the heat frizzes out my hair, and there is no radiance to it. It looks as though I'd been electrocuted. If summers are that hot, hell will be way too hot for me, and I love my hair healthy looking.

On a serious note, I love my soul, and God loves our souls much more than we do, so heaven is the place for us. It is not the will of God for us to perish. We can't save ourselves from the bottomless pit of fire unless we conform our wills to God's. To avoid such a disastrous eternity, let us first acknowledge God's Son. "Jesus said to him, 'I am the way, and the truth, and the life. No one comes to the Father except through me'" (John 14:6).

"Souled Out"

Giving your life to Christ means you are "souled out" to him. In most cultures. if you're "sold out," dog "nyaam" your supper. That's a Jamaican term that means if you're no longer with the norm, you have become the enemy. You could have been friends with someone, but then you "switched." SMH. When this happens in most communities, it's like radar has gone up for you, and when you come near the wrong "turf," you may be attacked.

Think of when you and a friend had a falling out; maybe you got a different job, or you two just outgrew each other. You're going to feel like a "sellout" because the norm has changed. You no longer see eye to eye; you no longer have common ground. You used to be close enough to someone to gossip about other people or date the same type of guys, but you got a degree and she didn't, or you got married and she didn't. Even though you want the best for the other person, he or she doesn't see it; he or she thinks you think you're superior, so you become enemies. Becoming a Christian can cause this; many start looking on new Christians as having "souled out" for Christ, and they feel threatened because they won't submit to God as well.

We grow up adapting to our norms, as we see others do. At some point, however, we realize we are always yearning for more than the world has to offer. There's war, but we want peace. There's gossip, but we want trust and honest relationships. There's hatred, but we want love. There's depression, darkness, loneliness, abuse, and insecurity, but we want happiness, friendship, light, and truth. We want to love and be loved. We don't want to abuse or be abused.

We were born to be happy and be in goodness at all times, but somewhere along the line, things went wrong. If you've ever read the Bible, you will know of this change in Genesis 3. Many of us are lucky enough to have experienced happiness and joy in spite of the forces of the world. There's a greater power than us—God—who has a great love for us and wants to rescue us. "You have overcome them: because greater is He that is within you, than he that is in the world" (1 John 4:4).

We receive so much from our Lord, but the world's influence can be so intense that we are blinded to the prize. It's like having a winning lotto ticket but being too distracted to check the numbers and learn we've won. We ponder our lack of spiritual wealth, but there's constant traffic in our head of things to do and not to do.

Satan does not want us to be free; he wants us in bondage to sin and fear. He is a deceiver who works through evil and darkness, and he gets people to lie to us about our freedom in Christ. People conspire to harm us, to destroy us, but no weapons formed against God's children will ever prosper. Christians want everyone to share in the same joy, peace, and freedom they've found in God; they want all to know the truth, Jesus Christ.

We are at times stricken with darkness and doubt; we find ourselves in the enemy's grip and concerned with just the things of this world. The enemy will continually use people and things to let us feel we've done something wrong by being "souled out." I love the lyrics from "Souled Out," by Hezekiah Walker: "I am 'souled out,' my mind is made up. Who can separate us from the love of Jesus? Not death or life." I have found joy, peace, grace, and favor in God. Today is the Lord's, and I can't change to please people, but I can change to please God. I have been transformed mentally, physically, emotionally, and spiritually for God, so when friends say, "Because you're a Christian, now you act like that," I answer boldly and pleasantly, "No, I'm a Christian now. I've souled out to God, so I can't do things that displease him."

I am happy being with God, knowing he has been with me no matter who I used to be. I pray you will find the same peace, joy, and love I have through him. You can if only you say, "Lord, forgive me for the things I have done, and come into my heart now as my Lord and personal Savior."

We Can All Rise Above

There's nothing wrong with the things you go through in life. The saying "Every dog has its day" means you will have times of good and bad; the only issue is how you will arise from your situations. Will you conform to your own understanding of things? Will you use witchcraft, as some do to try to determine why things happen to them? Will you be bitter because of what you have gone through? Will you use your goodness to bless others with kind words and prayer? Will you seek to understand why you go through events, life itself? Until you commit to God who was, is, and will be, you will be a dead person walking, and no witchcraft can change that.

I once worked as a school nurse. In the lunchroom one day, I overheard the principal asking a teacher's aide why she didn't consider becoming a teacher, and another staff member commented that she was good enough to become one. Her response was, "No, there's too much paperwork involved." Why do we sell ourselves short? We all have been given the greatest potential to be the best we can be, but we don't know it. We can become the best in life, but we often accept the least. I love the job teachers' aides do—don't get me wrong—it's just the aide's reluctance to consider promoting herself that startled me.

If we want to climb Mount Everest, we can do so by putting our minds to it and trusting God. If it has been done before, then we can also do it, and if it hasn't been done before, well, we can be the first. Let us not settle for stagnancy but strive to continually rise; it is in this way that we can inspire and influence others—family, friends, neighbors, everyone we meet.

If we want to be Christian role models, we have to get out of our comfort zones; we must take on tasks that will bring glory to God, whether it's advocating for children who are not allowed to worship in schools, or praying for someone who looks sad and lonely in the streets, or praying for neighbors. We can reach for and end up on any level we want if we don't allow self-limitation to stop us. We should rely on God, who accentuates self-worth and endless potential. If we want to represent God on earth, we have to be great and at our best, because God is great and always at his best.

Forgive My Gossip

I hear people gossip about others at times, and I've gossiped myself, but I've come to realize there is no hypocrisy in God's kingdom, and if that's where I want to end up, I will have to lose that luggage. When people are gossiping about others, I just ignore the talk, laugh it off, or give neutral answers. I think that if I can't say whatever I'm saying about a person behind his or her back to his or her face, I shouldn't be talking about that person at all.

It's best to talk upfront with the person if you have a problem with him or her, and it might be good to have a witness to your conversation if you feel you need a mediator or someone who shares your feelings. However, if the other person is boisterous and you yourself are a hothead, realize that you can't fight fire with fire, so you should pray about it first. Ask God for guidance and to speak for you so that the other person will receive your words well and that you will receive that person's words just as well. Pray to God to bring clarity and peace to the situation.

Let me share my experience with you. I used to have a somewhat pleasant relationship with a female cousin-in-law, but she had a falling out with a male cousin-in-law. Due to some derogatory allegations the male made about the female and her soon-to-be fiancé, the families involved were in a compromising situation; speaking to one side made the other side angry. It caused a rift in the family, and she decided she wouldn't attend any family gatherings he was attending, and she didn't.

I wondered how I could please both parties, knowing there are always two sides to a story. I wanted to reach out to her, so I called her after praying about it. Surprisingly, she was very pleasant. She mentioned she had no beef with me but because she has been hurt by the male cousin-in-law, someone she had trusted and loved, she wanted to take time away from the family. Thank God I was able to clear the air between her and the rest of the family. It has been a couple of months since that phone conversation, and she and I have been in frequent contact, thanks to God.

Dear God, release us from demonic holds and make our burdens light. Help us to hold on to you and your Word. Help us to be steadfast and remain under your wings. I know the enemy is gnawing at us constantly, taking the least little chance to bring us under his sway and make us let go of you.

Heal Us, Lord

I had a slew of headaches. I had no idea if it was my wig causing them or something else, but they hurt, and I prayed for a healing, just as God had healed the women who bled: "A woman was there who had been subject to bleeding for twelve years, but no one could heal her. She came up behind him [Jesus] and touched the edge of his cloak, and immediately her bleeding stopped" (Luke 8: 43).

God, you made the blind see. You have performed so many miracles, through Jesus Christ, through Peter, and through other disciples and followers of Jesus Christ. I'm puzzled by how we humans limit ourselves in spite of the power you give us once we trust in your name. When people are sick, why do we limit ourselves to pray for healing? We are so quick to give something the praise for it, as I gave my wig. We should praise the promise, not the problem. God healed, and he promises to heal. "Are any of you sick? You should call for the elders of the church to come and pray over you, anointing you with oil in the name of the Lord" (James 5:14).

Lord, we should just pray and believe through the healing you've given others that we can definitely heal others through you. If someone is undergoing surgery or is battling sickness, help us pray, believe, and trust you will heal. You are God of goodness who causes "heal-th." It is not your will for us to be unhealthy; you want us to be our best physically, mentally, emotionally, and of course spiritually, so don't let us be afraid and resort to witchcraft, or only medicine, but give us your guidance and miracles.

Yes, Lord, I know you work through health care teams, but I think people depend more on science than on you for answers, let alone healing. I know we should not judge people and think they must deserve it if they are sick. That's not true. I realize we are only judging, and, sadly, that's grounds for us in return to be judged. Forgive us, Lord.

Grant Us a Sense of Belonging, Lord

The world is so tiny, so microscopic, and the Internet, Skype, Facebook, and other examples of technology have helped make it so. They give us a sense of closeness to family and friends wherever they are.

However, one day, on my way to work, I was driving down Fifth Avenue in New York. I looked at stores such as *Wempe* and thought that someone like me couldn't afford to purchase even a pin in any of them. But who says? Why do we limit ourselves to wanting the "finer" things in life? What makes us think that we are not celebrities in our own right? It's as if we think we can't get there. Some things are costly, and we've grown accustomed to our own little communities where we feel a sense of belonging. But God, your Word says, "The earth is the Lord's, and everything in it, the world, and all who live in it" (Psalm 24:1). Help us realize that everything is available to us and that we should not limit ourselves, our dreams. The world is small, and our time is short. If we want something, all we have to do is pray, seek your validation and guidance, and go for it boldly.

Lest We Judge Others

It is good to be a part of a care group. It is a truthful way of expressing yourself and supplementing Sunday services. I know a lot of people associate Sunday as being God's, but every day is the Lord's. One night, at a care group meeting, I shared how my mind and spirit had been bothered for two days, ever since a friend of mine got into an altercation with another coworker. I hadn't been there, so I considered the other person to be in the wrong out of loyalty to my friend. This really bothered my spirit, so I asked God what to do and where to get information in the Bible about what was happening to me. Just as a singer tells a story or offers insight through song, God, through his Word, gives us information that will guide us.

When you need a question answered or to discover the reason for any emotions you are experiencing—love, hate, depression, forgiveness—turn to the back of the Bible; it will give you Scriptures regarding any question.

I prayed, and God told me to read James, which pierced my heart. "My brothers and sisters, believers in our glorious Lord Jesus Christ must not show favoritism. Suppose a man comes into your meeting wearing a gold ring and fine clothes, and a poor man in filthy old clothes also comes in. If you show special attention to the man wearing fine clothes and say, 'Here's a good seat for you' but say to the poor man, 'You stand there' or 'Sit on the floor by my feet,' have you not discriminated among yourselves and become judges with evil thoughts?" (James 2:1–4).

I was so elated by how clearly this Scripture related to what I was going through. God often encourages us to read passages and do things, but we disobey. We are all in a maze, and God is looking down at us, telling us which way to go and what to do next. He leads us through some challenging turns that we could not figure out for ourselves, but God is a true God who sees and understands the maze we are in. If we just ask him for his help, his answers to our questions, we will gain peace, and we won't have to be afraid or embarrassed for winning the battle.

Dear God, at points in our mazes, we've fallen short many times, but we thank you for continually delivering us.

Isn't it just arrogant human nature that causes us to judge? I remember a woman in her late forties who had undergone *in vitro* fertilization to give birth to multiples. She did not have any paternal support, or any support for that manner. I wondered why she wanted to do this to herself.

One day, one of her newborns became very ill and required multiple surgeries, so my coworkers and I joined in prayer for the infant. I have to beg for forgiveness because I was not offering humble acceptance; I felt that the mother had brought this on herself. I even refrained from saying hello to her, because I could not understand why she would put herself in such a situation.

A couple of weeks after that, however, I saw her and became more empathetic. I realized that it is not for us to judge; we should not assume things about people and their situations but should ask God for guidance and understanding. "Speak and act as those who are going to be judged by the law that gives freedom, because judgment without mercy will be shown to anyone who has not been merciful. Mercy triumphs over judgment" (James 2:12–14).

Lord, I beg for forgiveness because I have judged. I had no mercy on this mother. I ask you to forgive me. Your Word has given me knowledge and has helped me to be merciful, to judge righteously, and not show favoritism. "Stop judging by mere appearances, and make a right judgment" (John 7:24).

I remember one young mother who had premature twins, one of whom died. The young mother had the support of her family, including her grandmother, who I think was gay; she dressed like a man and had a very masculine demeanor. I wondered why the young mother had suffered the loss of her child. There were complicating medical factors, but I couldn't help wonder if it was due to disobedience in her family. "He punishes the children and their children for the sin of the fathers to the third and fourth generation" (Exodus 34).

Help Us Become Your Messengers, Lord

We Christians are not the message but the messengers. The worst part about acting against God is being disobedient. The best thing is in the message and its offer of a joyous, true, and acceptable life. It's never too late, because God always loves us.

God, we disobey you by lying, even though you command us not to lie. We disobey you in abusing our children physically, mentally, and sexually. We disobey you by being homosexuals, adulterers, fornicators, thieves, and murderers; we act against you in so many ways. We also pass these acts and behaviors on to our children, because children live what they see.

Deep down, many of us don't want our children to be like us or to live the lives we are living because we have a sense that we are not living totally right. We should check ourselves; those of us who don't take into account what I am saying should take account what God has said.

Even if we live our lives as we want, even if we are not true messengers of God, we can still become familiar with what the Bible tells us all. Many of us refuse to learn about God's Word because we fear we won't measure up to it, but none of us is perfect. The important thing is that we start to learn God's Word; he will help us finish.

At times when we sin, we can say, "Oops—but no one saw, no one knows, so everything's okay." Okay what? Are we free to sin again? To abuse, hurt, neglect, and live as our flesh desires? God knows our lives from start to finish, from womb to tomb. God is slow to anger; he is the best Father ever. He gives us multiple chances and plenty of time to get our acts together, but the time to get it together is right now; this book will pierce us all with the truth that God loves us. "For God so loved the world that he gave his one and only Son, that whoever believes in him shall not perish but have eternal life" (John 3:16).

We are never the best messengers of God we can be, but we always have another chance to turn away from places in the maze our Father doesn't want us to go and avoid dead ends in the maze. "For the wages of sin is death, but the gift of God is eternal life in Christ Jesus our Lord" (Romans 6:23).

Let's walk free from darkness and all that takes us from God. Imagine being in prison for years upon years, struggles upon struggles, heartaches upon heartaches, but hitting that exit door, feeling the sun on our faces, and smelling freedom. We would never want to go back to our old worlds.

We, however, are in the world of sin. We are in jail because we broke the law, but there all types of people in jail; some work on their GEDs while others gang bang, and some feel they are there because they were wrongfully convicted. We can compare the whole world to this prison setting; if you are in prison for a crime you did or did not commit, just as we come into this world born in sin, then some sins we did or did not commit, but we all have Original Sin from Adam and Eve.

You can get the Word of God growing up learning it or picking it up by bits and pieces here and there. Here, you are getting it from this book, and this allows you to examine yourself in the same way being incarcerated can offer you a reality check. You can use the Word to guide you and get out of prison on good terms. You may not be able to get out of your circumstances, just as some can't escape generational curses because of what their ancestors have done. You can, however, pray to God and stay close to him, fast and pray for miracles, and hope we may ultimately live and not die.

We receive deliverance when we stay close to God, and we are reassured that we are free from eternal death. Just as prisoners can finally be freed, we should ask God for freedom from generational curses.

Set us free, Lord, and help us to not be judged unfairly, as many inmates are. Help us so that after freedom, we'll continue to pray and converse with you. Lead us, Lord, and not just us, but also our children and our children's children, in Jesus' name, amen.

Revenge Is the Lord's

At times, Lord, we feel the need to just bust out and put people in their places by cursing them, but we know you don't approve of that, Lord. We know there are times when we just have to rebuke people. "As for those who persist in sin, rebuke them in the presence of all, so that the rest may stand in fear" (1 Timothy 5:20). Lord, you have told us, "Do not take revenge dear friends, but leave room for God's wrath, for it is written: 'It is mine to avenge: I will repay,' says the Lord" (Romans 12:19). If we lash out against people who harm us, it will be a bloody battle. People who have done us "somethangs" provide us with what to say to them if anything at all, and how to say it.

Have you ever had the feeling of being half-embarrassed and half-glad? It happened to me one morning when I was called at 7:47 a.m. to fill in for a nurse at a school at 8:00 a.m. I had to drop my son off at his school, and I tried to call to say I had gotten the assignment late but was on my way, but the number I had been given was out of service. I called the district supervisor to check in at a certain time and said that I was at the school, which was dishonest; I hadn't gotten there yet. On the one hand, I felt I was not being dishonest because through what she said, I could tell she assumed I was there, and I did not object.

At times, we tend to lie indirectly, say, by not correcting something that's not true, by playing along so we look "right." Help us not to do this, Lord, because this is being deceitful, and you are a true and honest God who despises deceit.

I finally reached the school, but the main office staffers were very upset that I was late. They didn't believe that I had missed the exit on the highway and had had a tough time finding parking; I actually had to double park. They reported me to the district supervisor and my agency. Who was to blame? Obviously, me. I had arrived late and hadn't successfully called in. After I hurried up and administered morning medication to students, I rushed out to find a parking spot for my car and get back as soon as possible. The school called the district supervisor a second time to report I had left the building for a long time and had not returned.

I felt so frustrated that I wanted to confront someone. I boldly went into the school's office and asked three staff members, "Why would you guys do such a thing?" One said that she wasn't the one who had called the district supervisor, but I knew someone had, because my immediate supervisor called to question why I had left the building.

I felt so angry, and I really wanted to go home, because they obviously had no empathy for me, who was just trying to park my car and avoid a ticket. My blood was really boiling, and I went back and forth with the staff about how inconsiderate they had been. I honestly wanted to be professional and civil, but at times, people just pull your string and bring out the "woof woof" in you. I hadn't had the correct number to let the school know I was going to be late—it was just a crazy morning.

We've all experienced one of those mornings, days, or nights. I asked God to rectify the situation; people of God do not want to leave others with bad tastes in their mouths about us. I was supposed to be a bold, honest example of God, and I know I had communicated wrong and did not allow God Almighty to guide me and keep me mindful and humble. I had let my emotions lead me, and I wasn't expected to be allowed to work at that school again. There were hundreds of other schools I could work at, but I had brought unfavorable light on myself as a Christian and as a professional and on my agency.

We go through bigger altercations than this at work, home, church, and elsewhere, but we must pray to God to help us be obedient, dependable, and slow to anger. "My dear brothers and sisters, take note of this: Everyone should be quick to listen, slow to speak and slow to become angry, because human anger does not produce the righteousness that God desires. Therefore get rid of all moral filth and evil that is so prevalent and humbly accept the word planted in you, which can save you" (James 1:19–21).

We have to pray to the Lord for forgiveness when we behave in such a manner. I swallowed my pride and apologized to the lady. She thought it was a communication issue and seemed very receptive to my apology. This taught me to redirect my energy positively to these children and humbly pray that they'd be healed of ADHD, autism, or whatever they had been diagnosed with.

Stand for Holiness

"Jesus answered, 'Truly, truly, I say to you, unless one is born of water and the Spirit, he cannot enter the kingdom of God'" (John 3:5). My husband tells me that love is his religion, but I say that love is not a religion but an emotion. In Christianity, we can find love, peace, joy, and other emotions, but we have to stand for holiness. I tell him that many people have gone under and are still struggling with things that are not pleasing to God, but accepting Christ is a process. We first become like a child who slowly grows in a godly way. We learn that our aim should be to please God. We are not perfect, but his grace will carry us through, so accepting Christ is a process.

"And he said: 'Truly I tell you, unless you change and become like little children, you will never enter the kingdom of heaven'"(Matthew 18:3). I can recall when I answered Christ and gave my life to him. A few days before I did, I wanted to talk to a pastor at church. On my way to see her, the Devil said to me, "If you become a Christian, I will take your husband from you." I can still hear it loud and clear. This made me felt very afraid; I didn't want to lose my husband. As soon as I reached Pastor Joy's office, I shared my experience with her, and then and there she prayed for me; she rebuked the Devil and reminded him that he was a liar and that the blood of Jesus Christ was against him. I was very thankful for her prayer, because prayer changes things. It's the one weapon we have against the enemy, so we'd best not fail to use it.

I also felt ashamed of giving my life to God at first. I wondered what my friends would think. I thought I couldn't go clubbing or partying anymore, and I felt that I would have to let go of so much. However, again I realized that the enemy was a liar who didn't want to lose a soul. If we are not with God, we are with the Devil.

We Cannot Obey Two Masters

My grandmother always used to tell us that we couldn't serve two masters at the same time, and how I wondered as a child what she was talking about! Now, as an adult in a walk with God, I realize how important it is for me to make a stand on good and evil. I took a stance, and in April 2009, I was water baptized by Pastor Benjamin in Bronx Bethany Church of The Nazarene in New York. I felt a sense of newness, but it wasn't an immediate transformation into a "holier than thou" attitude; rather, I felt I was on my way to goodness, to greatness, and to what the Lord had in store for my life, which in reality is his. Can I get an Amen? Amen!

I am not the best at praying for myself or others, or staying committed to Christ, or even tithing, but his grace is sufficient to make me what he wants me to be. In the years after my baptism, I learned more about God, how to pray, and how to stay committed to God. I remember thinking that my little prayers were not powerful, but Paul wrote to Timothy that God does not give the spirit of fear but of power, love, and a sound mind.

Tithing

If Christ is within us, through him and because of him we can do anything, and we have his power to do so. I remember a coworker asking, "Why should I give what little money I have to God?" I thought to myself of the millions of people who think like that. How can the church grow if we don't contribute to it? We can find a million and one reasons not to tithe but still spend $15, $25, even $40 every Friday or Saturday night to defile our bodies, get drunk, dodge bullets, or get in fights. The club owner has to pay the artists, the DJ, the photographer, and all other expenses, right? Well, the church has expenses as well; it serves the community and caters to lost souls, so we should not rob God of what is required of us; one-tenth of what we earn is his, so if we make $20, $2 is his.

"Will a man rob God? Yet you rob me. But you ask, 'How do we rob you?' In the tithes and offerings. You are under a curse—the whole nation of you—because you are robbing me. Bring the whole tithe into the storehouse, that there may be food in my house. 'Test me in this,' says the Lord Almighty, 'and see if I will not throw open the floodgates of heaven and pour out so much blessing that you will not have room enough for it'" (Malachi 3:8–10). Wow, how much blessings we will receive when we pay God first!

At first, I thought as well that I didn't have to give. I had tons of misunderstandings about tithing and many other aspects of Christianity. However, through continual reading of the Bible, praying, and having relationships with Christians and non-Christians, I've learned, I've grown, and I'm still growing. God made us in his image to live truthful, happy, and peaceful lives, but if we are not in agreement with him by making it known we love and want to follow him and him alone, we are at the Devil's disposal.

Traveling with God

I thank God for rescuing me. I thank him for his mercy. Even when I was not 100 percent with him, he continued to have mercy and be 100 percent with me. Even though I was not doing right, he made righteousness available to me. The lead pastor at my church once preached a sermon about how if we are neither hot nor cold, we are like the sea—we go wherever the wind blows us. This is true; this is why we are confused, depressed, and hurt; this is why we lie, steal, cheat, and otherwise rebel against the Creator.

How long shall we be like this? We are the drivers of our lives; we steer the wrong way, we get flats, we run out of gas, and we crash at times because we don't read the road signs, the Word of God. We do not care for any other drivers on the road. Some of us have empty cars, nothing to hold on to, and some of us have luggage packed all the way up to the front seat and can't see where we're going.

Stop! We should think of how we can give our excess luggage to God, fix our cars, and not worry about gas, which Jesus will provide. We can let go of the wheel and find peace in being chauffeured. How pleasant it is to have a navigation system to eternity for us and our families! "And they said, 'Believe in the Lord Jesus, and you will be saved, you and your household'" (Acts 16:31). When we take a stand

and are saved, our spouses, our brothers and sisters, our children, and our parents will take us for true examples of peace and mercy and will eventually follow us, sincere examples of Christians.

If we let God chauffeur us, our baggage will be light, our hearts will be free of burdens, and our sins will be forgiven; heaven will rejoice and hover over us. Otherwise, as in the Steven Seagal movie, we will be "Marked for Death." Wishy-washy people don't get into heaven, and the bottomless pit is filled with fury. Just as vultures seek and devour dead meat, the Devil hunts to devour souls. When Jesus is on our side, we will be crowned with life; the Devil will be unsuccessful; he knows when God is around, and he knows not to mess with God's children. "You believe that there is one God. That's fine! Even the demons believe that and tremble with fear" (James 2:19).

Make your call today; answer the call to accept Christ as your personal Savior so there will be no misunderstanding about whom you belong to. You will not regret it.

I love you, Lord, and I'm glad I made my stance.

Christianity Is a Great Reward

Many people think being Christian is a mushy thing to do, but that's a lie. It's the most rewarding thing they could do. Some hide in their sins and think they will be able to commit them forever, but that's a lie as well. Many feel guilty and unworthy for what they have done or are tempted to do. I pray they will live not for themselves but for God and the goodness he has in store for them.

I remember my perceptions about Christians before I became one; I thought Christians were boring, old-fashioned people who couldn't have fun or be spontaneous. I thought I'd rather have fun, do anything I wanted while I was young, and get baptized when I was old. When people preached to me about giving my life to God before judgment day, it would just go over my head.

I realize now that the enemy had been lying to me when he said that I could live as I wished until the trumpet sounded on judgment day, when I could run and get baptized then. Can you imagine a greater lie than that?

If I could change one thing about how people view others, I would teach them that it is others' hearts that matter, not their clothes or hairstyles or manners of speech. What is important is that they serve God. "Rend your heart and not your garments. Return to the LORD your God, for he is gracious and compassionate, slow to anger and abounding in love, and he relents from sending calamity" (Joel 2:13). I came to know God even though I had bleached-blonde hair, wore makeup, ripped jeans, polka-dot blouse, and sported well-manicured nails; I have come to realize that these things don't matter to him. As long as my heart is clean and my mind, body, and soul are his, then, like Bugs Bunny says, "That's all, folks!"

At times, I want to go to nightclubs, but only when the "pawty's dun," when the party is over. I want to show up to give young women a Bible or a word from God. We Christians have to seek out where these young women are if we want to help them know God and realize one day that the things they want to do are not God's will, that they have to obey God's will to gain eternal peace and happiness. I have nothing against good times and celebrating; I've been there myself. We know hard-core parties go on with girls "gyrating" on trees or on light structures in clubs. We've all been to compromising places, but if Jesus Christ were standing in front of us right now, would he be happy or displeased with us? The answer to that question should make us stop forever or continue forever our behavior, because we all have a sense of right and wrong.

If you try to turn around God's way and Word, you will be in big trouble. I can understand if you have no knowledge of his Word, but if you know it and dismiss it, you are refusing to be informed of the past, present, and future. This results in a wishy-washy approach—you will have nothing substantial to hold on to.

Obeying God's Instructions

Pastor Creflo Dollar preached on TV about giving God space in your life so he could give you instructions, and that could be, for instance, even giving someone your car. Many mouths dropped at this. "My what?" Remember, though, that Peter gave the net to Jesus when he was unable to catch any fish, and what happened? The net ended up so full that they could hardly pull it onboard.

We have to be obedient. I learned in Sunday school, "Obedience is the very best way to show that you believe, doing exactly what the Lord commands, and doing it happily." We will find out for a fact that when we trust and obey God and give him a place in our lives, he will instruct and bless us.

Lord, I can't help think of how I wanted to host an I Love My Sister meeting at my apartment, a desire you placed in my spirit, and how on that day at the Global Summit, you told me to tell young women like me how great you are and what you've done for me. I obeyed; I invited a bunch of women from my Facebook page, my cell phone contacts, and ended up successful. I Love My Sister empowers women to live their best lives ever and to share their experiences with anything—their relationships with others, their walks with God, and so forth.

Lord, we women know we often "hate" on each other at first sight; we put up walls before we even know each other. We hope to break down those walls, letting women realize that when we share with each other, we can turn our trials into triumphs, we can become victors instead of victims, we can turn our messes into messages, and we can change our tests into testimonies. "He comforts us in all our troubles so that we can comfort others. When they are troubled, we will be able to give them the same comfort God has given us" (2 Corinthians 1:4). Hallelujah, I Love My Sister has become a success and will continue to empower women one step at a time, even in our stilettos.

Let Us Be God's Ambassadors

I and many of the other women can attest to the fact that we've become more submissive to God. I've gotten a conscience and a peace no one can understand. I am an ambassador for Christ; I feel the need to do what God asks of me regardless of the cost; I believe that even though things may seem impossible, if we do our part, God will take care of the rest. When we don't work for Christ, our souls will feel lost, and we will experience darkness and confusion. When we do work on his behalf, we bare goodness unconditionally, always feel happy, and know our purpose. We also feel the need to help not just ourselves but also others. Many may use the words *goodwill*, *Christianity*, or *religion* loosely, but my sisters and I don't.

We should all ask ourselves, Have we lived to please God as humans and as Christians? "Religion that God our Father accepts as pure and faultless is this: to look after orphans and widows in their distress and to keep oneself from being polluted by the world" (James 1:27).